MYSTERIES OF METEORS, ASTEROIDS, AND COMETS

by Ellen Labrecque

CAPSTONE PRESS
a capstone imprint

Capstone Captivate is published by Capstone Press, an imprint of Capstone.
1710 Roe Crest Drive
North Mankato, Minnesota 56003
www.capstonepub.com

Copyright © 2021 by Capstone. All rights reserved. No part of this publication may be reproduced in whole or in part, or stored in a retrieval system, or transmitted in any form or by any means, electronic, mechanical, photocopying, recording, or otherwise, without written permission of the publisher.

Library of Congress Cataloging-in-Publication Data is available on the Library of Congress website.

ISBN: 978-1-4966-8077-8 (library binding)
ISBN: 978-1-4966-8716-6 (paperback)
ISBN: 978-1-4966-8170-6 (eBook PDF)

Summary: Describes meteors, asteroids, and comets, their histories, and unsolved mysteries about them.

Image Credits
Alamy Stock Photo: NG Images, 28; AP Images: P Video, 15; Dreamstime: Bazuzzza, 17; iStock: Marharyta Marko, 5, serpeblu, 4; NASA: ESA/ATG medialab, 13, ESA/Giotto Project, 23, ESA/STScI, 25, JPL-Caltech, 9, 27, JPL-Caltech/Teledyne, 11, JPL-Caltech/UCAL/MPS/DLR/IDA, 12, NASA Goddard, 29; Newscom: Danita Delimont Photography/David Wall, 22; Pixabay: Hans, 8; Shutterstock: abriendomundo, 19, Aygun Ali, background, Dotted Yeti, 16, faboi, 18, Johan Swanepoel, 6, solarseven, 21, Song_about_summer, 14

Editorial Credits
Editor: Hank Musolf; Designer: Sara Radka; Media Researcher: Jo Miller;
Production Specialist: Laura Manthe

All internet sites appearing in back matter were available and accurate when this book was sent to press.

Printed in the United States 4867

TABLE OF CONTENTS

SMASHING INTO EARTH 4

DEFENDING PLANET EARTH 8

ASTEROIDS 12

METEOROIDS, METEORS, AND METEORITES 16

COMETS 20

FROM FAR AWAY 24

WHAT IS STILL A MYSTERY? 26

GLOSSARY 30

READ MORE 31

INTERNET SITES 31

INDEX 32

Words in **bold** are in the glossary.

CHAPTER 1

SMASHING INTO EARTH

Imagine Earth 66 million years ago. The sun is shining. Dinosaurs are stomping around. An **asteroid** is hurtling toward the planet. It is the size of a mountain. It is traveling at 40,000 miles (64,370 kilometers) per hour! The asteroid looks like a giant fireball as it gets closer. It burns much hotter than the sun. It explodes on impact. The crash is felt all over the world. The impact sends a blanket of dust into the air. The sky becomes black. Soon dinosaurs are wiped out forever.

Scientists believe dinosaurs were wiped out by an asteroid.

An asteroid flies toward a planet.

Scientists believe dinosaurs died out after a large asteroid hit Earth. Today, outer space is filled with asteroids like this one. Could a rock like this hit Earth again? It could, but don't worry. The chances of a large asteroid hitting Earth are very small. People also watch space objects every day to help keep us safe.

Outer space is filled with asteroids and other objects. They include small rocks called **meteoroids** and objects made of rock, ice, and dust called **comets**. We know a lot about these objects, but scientists are still learning about them. They are solving mysteries about them as they learn.

MYSTERY FACT

The asteroid that scientists believe wiped out the dinosaurs was more than 6 miles (9.7 km) wide.

Outer space is filled with flying rocks. Most **astronomers** think the **Big Bang** is the way the universe began. About 13.7 billion years ago, all the **matter** and **energy** in outer space was crammed in a small, hot place. The pressure was so intense that it finally burst. It exploded in every direction. This led to the planets, moons, and stars forming. Scientists think it is also the reason we have so many rocks in space.

MYSTERY FACT

Our universe continues to expand today. When the universe grows, galaxies spread farther apart. Scientists are still trying to figure out how fast the universe expands.

CHAPTER 2

DEFENDING PLANET EARTH

Astronomers study space rocks. The space rocks tell the story of our universe. The ones closest to Earth are called Near Earth Objects (NEOs). Over 19,000 NEOs have been discovered. More than 30 new ones are found every week. Astronomers keep track of them. Most of them are at least 30 million miles (48 million km) away. Some are closer.

Potentially Hazardous Objects (PHOs) are as close as 4.7 million miles (7.5 million km). Astronomers keep an especially close eye on PHOs.

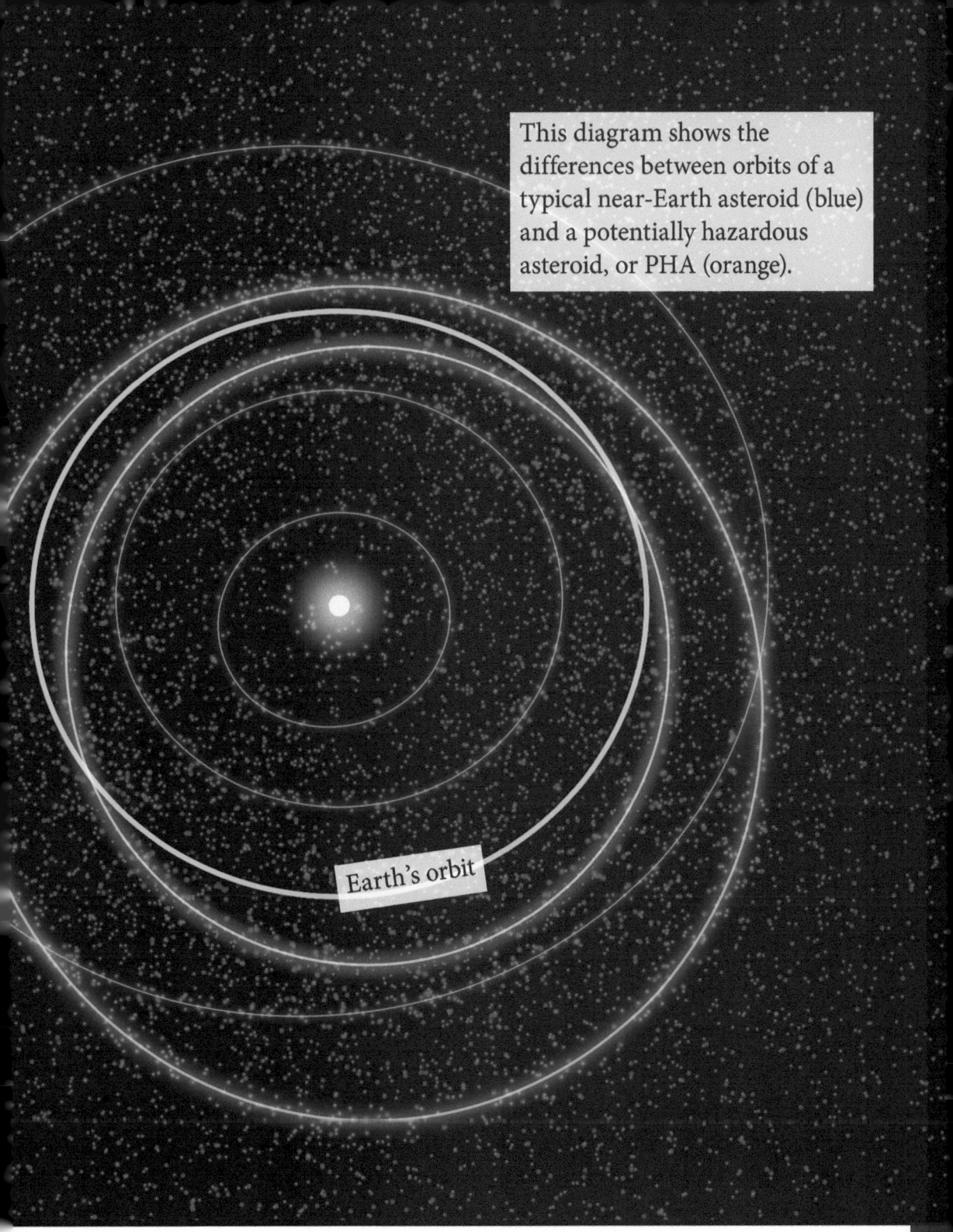

This diagram shows the differences between orbits of a typical near-Earth asteroid (blue) and a potentially hazardous asteroid, or PHA (orange).

The Planetary Defense Coordination Office is one group working to keep us safe. Group members track space objects that are flying close to Earth. They are building a new asteroid-hunting **telescope** called the NEOCam. It will be ready in 2024.

The NEOCam sensor (right) is the foundation for the proposed Near Earth Object Camera, or NEOCam (left).

Asteroids give off heat against the backdrop of cold space. This telescope will be able to pick up that heat. The more we know about asteroids, the better prepared we can be.

CHAPTER 3

ASTEROIDS

Asteroids are called small planets. Like our planets, they orbit the sun. Most asteroids can be found in the **asteroid belt**. The asteroid belt is a place between the planets Mars and Jupiter. More than 2 million asteroids are found there. The brightest asteroid in the sky is named Vesta. The biggest asteroid ever found is named Ceres. It is more than 590 miles (900 km) wide!

Vesta

Dwarf planet Ceres is located in the main asteroid belt between the orbits of Mars and Jupiter.

Asteroids crash into Earth every day. Together, the space rocks that fall daily weigh close to 200,000 pounds (91,000 kilograms). These rocks aren't the big kind that could really hurt us. Earth is surrounded by thin layers of gases. This is called an **atmosphere**. Our atmosphere serves as a shield. It breaks up asteroids into pieces. They usually reach Earth in the form of dust and small rocks.

Earth seen from space at night

Throughout Earth's long history, gigantic rocks have hit us. We have the **craters** to prove it. The biggest crater on Earth is called Vredefort Crater. It is in South Africa. It is 190 miles (305 km) wide. An asteroid created this crater 2 billion years ago. It was at least 6 miles (9.6 km) wide.

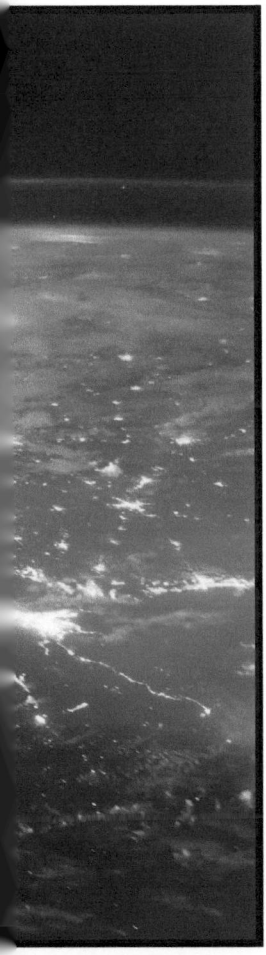

AN UNEXPECTED ASTEROID

In 2013, astronomers were caught off guard. A giant asteroid entered Earth's atmosphere above Chelyabinsk, Russia. The asteroid was 55 feet (17 meters) wide and more than 26 million pounds (11 million kg). Astronomers didn't see it coming. The asteroid was bright and flying close to the sun. Luckily, it exploded before it hit the ground. The air blast still caused damage to more than 7,000 buildings. Thankfully, nobody died.

CHAPTER 4

METEOROIDS, METEORS, AND METEORITES

Asteroids and meteoroids are made of the same kind of rock and metals. They are both found outside of our atmosphere. A meteoroid is a much smaller asteroid. It can be as small as a pebble. Many times a meteoroid is just a piece of asteroid. Two asteroids might have crashed into each other, causing pieces to break off.

ASTEROID
COMET
METEOR SHOWER
METEORITE

Shooting stars can be seen in the sky on a clear night.

When a meteoroid enters our atmosphere, it becomes known as a **meteor**, or a shooting star. This happens when our atmosphere can't deflect the meteoroid. Instead, it causes the meteoroid to slow down suddenly. It usually burns up before it hits our surface. This burning causes a bright streak across a dark sky. Sometimes the meteor doesn't burn up. It actually lands on Earth. What remains is called a **meteorite**. Most of the time the meteorites are so small that we don't even notice them.

meteorite

CHAPTER 5

COMETS

Comets are another type of space object. Comets form far away from the sun. They are made up of ice, dust, and rock. Comets are nicknamed "dirty snowballs." Some comets are only a couple of feet wide. Others are miles across. Many comets can be found in distant outer space. This region is called the **Oort Cloud**. It is trillions of miles away from the sun and cold. This keeps the comets icy. But if a comet comes closer to the sun, it begins to warm up.

The Oort Cloud is a region that many comets can be found in.

Comet McNaught, Ashburton, South Island, New Zealand

When a comet begins to warm up from the sun, its icy parts turn into gases mixed with dust. These gases reflect the light from the sun. They form long, bright tails. These tails stretch for millions of miles across space. When comets come close enough to Earth, we can see them. These comets light up the sky.

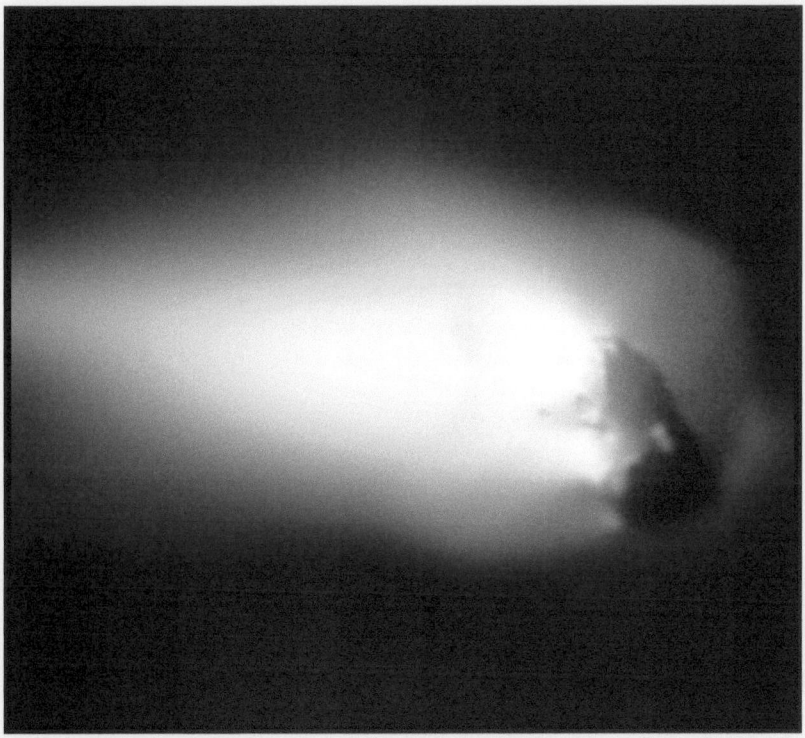

HALLEY'S COMET

Halley's Comet is the world's most famous comet. It is one of the only comets we can see with our naked eyes. Halley's Comet orbits the sun every 76 years. The next time we will see it is in 2061.

CHAPTER 6

FROM FAR AWAY

In 2017, a mysterious object was discovered floating in space. It was like nothing that had ever been seen in our solar system before. That's because it was actually from another solar system! Scientists named the space object 'Oumuamua. Scientists believe it is mostly made of rock. It had been traveling for millions of years until it reached us. 'Oumuamua was the first object from another solar system to appear in ours. Scientists don't know exactly where it came from. Scientists can learn a lot about other solar systems by studying it.

'Oumuamua was spotted 15 million miles (24 million km) from Earth.

CHAPTER 7

WHAT IS STILL A MYSTERY?

Scientists are still looking for answers about meteors and meteorites. They believe meteorites could help us understand the beginning of our solar system. Astronomers work every day to learn more about space and all its speeding space rocks. They study fossils of asteroids that landed on Earth a long time ago. These could provide more evidence for the origins of the universe. Studying space objects that landed on Earth can also tell us more about our planet. Scientists have wondered if the water on Earth could have been from an icy comet. But no one knows for sure yet.

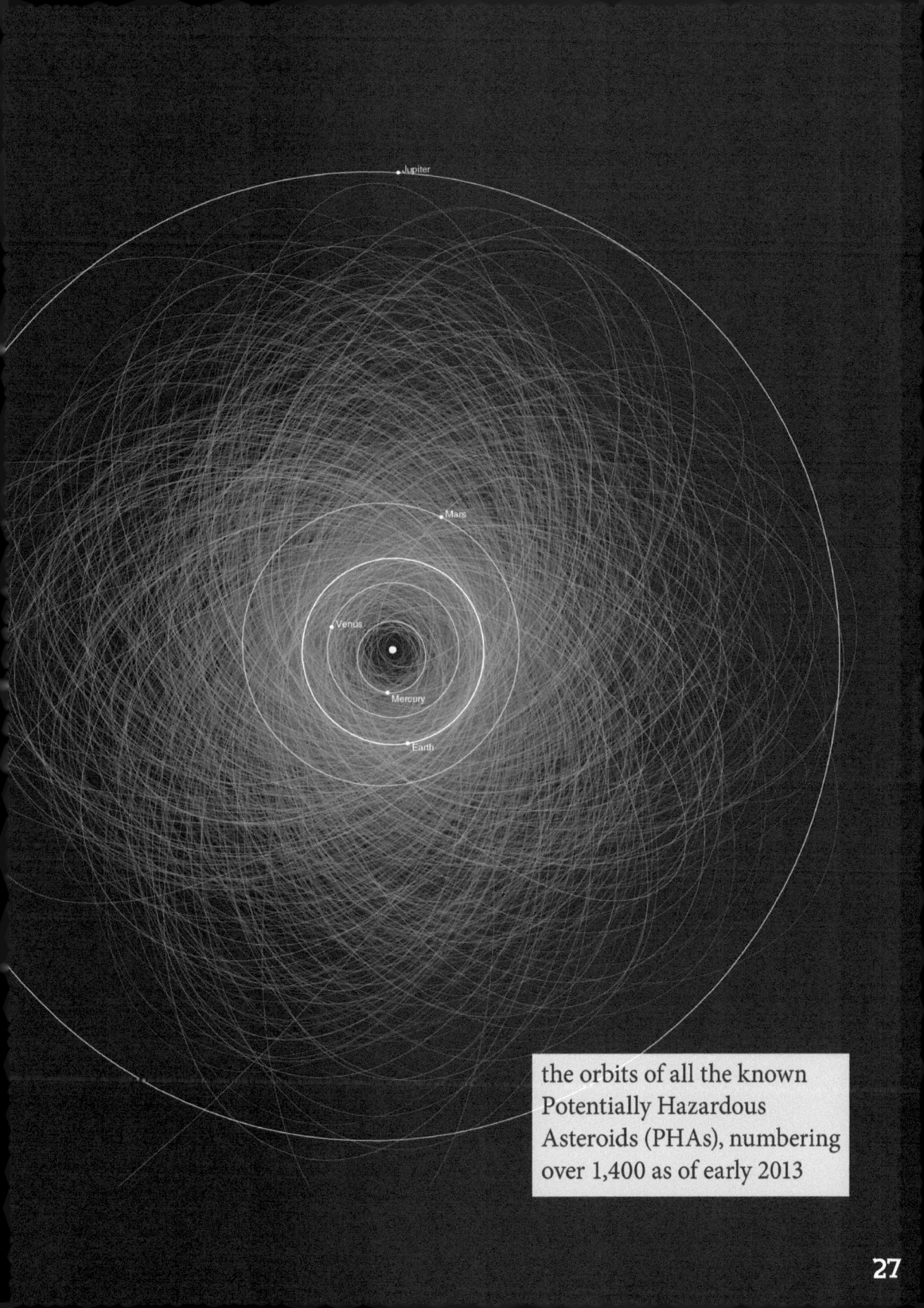

the orbits of all the known Potentially Hazardous Asteroids (PHAs), numbering over 1,400 as of early 2013

Scientists have formed groups to track asteroids that might hit Earth.

Could an asteroid ever hit Earth again? Could it cause real damage? The short answer is yes. But it is very unlikely. Astronomers are working to figure out how to stop an asteroid, especially a giant one on a direct path to Earth. No known asteroid is set to hit our planet in the next 100 years. The next chance for an asteroid to hit Earth is 2185. The asteroid is named Bennu. Astronomers are watching it closely. Still, Bennu only has a one in 2,700 chance of making impact. That is not even a 1 percent chance! *Phew!*

Astronomers also continue to study the objects that pass through our solar system. We could learn how different other solar systems are from our own. Learning about them could help us understand our solar system better as well. In the meantime, there is one thing we know for sure: We are just beginning to understand the mysteries of space. And space certainly rocks!

Asteroid Bennu

GLOSSARY

asteroid (AS-tuh-roid)—rocky object in space

asteroid belt (AS-tuh-roid belt)—the region of space between Mars and Jupiter where most asteroids are

astronomer (uh-STRON-uh-mer)—someone who studies outer space

atmosphere (AT-muh-sfeer)—gases that surround a planet or other objects in space

Big Bang (BIG BANG)—a theory that explains how the universe was formed

comet (KOM-it)—an object in space that that has dust and gas around it that may form a tail

crater (KREY-ter)—a cup-shaped hole in a planet or moon

energy (EN-er-jee)—any source of usable power

matter (MAT-er)—anything that occupies space

meteor (MEE-tee-er)—a meteorid that has entered Earth's atmosphere

meteorite (MEE-tee-er-rahyt)—a meteoroid that has reached Earth

meteoroid (MEE-tee-er-roid)—small body of rock traveling through space

Oort Cloud (ort kloud)—a far region in outer space where a lot of comets are

telescope (TEL-uh-skope)—a tool people use to look at objects in space

READ MORE

Gifford, Clive. *Super Space Encyclopedia.* New York: DK Publishing, 2019.

Kurtz, Kevin. *Comets and Asteroids in Action: An Augmented Reality Experience.* Minneapolis: Lerner Publishing, 2020.

Trefil, James, and Buzz Aldrin. *Space Atlas, Second Edition: Mapping the Universe and Beyond.* Washington, D.C.: National Geographic, 2018.

INTERNET SITES

NASA Science
science.nasa.gov

National Geographic: Asteroids and Comets
www.nationalgeographic.com/science/space/solar-system/asteroids-comets/

National Science Foundation
www.nsf.gov

INDEX

asteroid belt, 12
asteroid impact, 4, 14, 29
asteroid speed, 4
astronomers, 7, 8, 15, 26, 29
atmosphere, 14

Bennu, 29
Big Bang, 7

Ceres, 12
comets, 5, 20, 23, 26
craters, 15

dinosaurs, 4, 5

energy, 7

Jupiter, 12

Mars, 12
matter, 7
meteorite, 19, 26
meteoroids, 5, 16, 19

Near Earth Objects (NEOs), 8

Oort Cloud, 20
'Oumuamua, 24

Planetary Defense Coordination Office, 10
Potentially Hazardous Objects (PHOs), 8

Russia, 15

scientists, 5, 7, 24, 26
South Africa, 15

telescopes, 10, 11

universe expansion, 7

Vesta, 12
Vredefort Crater, 15